Watching the Weather

Dew and Frost

Elizabeth Miles

Heinemann Library
Chicago, Illinois

Designed by Richard Parker and Celia Jones
Illustrations by Jeff Edwards
Originated by Dot Gradations
Printed and bound in China by South China Printing Company

09 08 07
10 9 8 7 6 5 4 3

Library of Congress Cataloging-in-Publication Data
Miles, Elizabeth, 1960-
    Dew and frost / Elizabeth Miles.
        p. cm. -- (Watching the weather)
Includes bibliographical references and index.
ISBN 1-4034-5576-7 (HC), 1-4034-5674-7 (Pbk.)
ISBN 978-1-4034-5576-5 (HC), 978-1-4034-5674-8 (Pbk.)
1. Dew--Juvenile literature. 2. Frost--Juvenile literature. I. Title. II. Series.
QC929.D5M55 2005
551.57'44--dc22

                            2004002363

Acknowledgments
The author and publisher are grateful to the following for permission to reproduce copyright material: Getty Images/Image Bank; Getty Images/PhotoDisc p. i; Alamy Images pp. 4, 5, 15, 17, 20, 21, 27; Comstock p. 11; Corbis/Craig Tuttle p. 7; Corbis/Douglas Peebles p. 16; Corbis/Ecoscene/Andrew Brown p. 19; Corbis/Galen Rowell p. 25; Corbis/Michael Busselle p. 8; Corbis/Lee Cohen p. 23; Getty images/Photodisc pp. 9, 12; Harcourt Education Ltd/Tudor Photography pp. 28, 29; NHPA/Anthony Bannister p. 14; OSF/Olivier Grunewald p. 26; Photofusion/Paul Risdale p. 13; Powerstock/Paco Elvira p. 18; SPL/Astrid & Hans-Frieder Michler p. 24; Travel Ink p. 10.

Cover photographs of dew and frost reproduced with permission of Getty Images/Image Bank; Getty Images/PhotoDisc.

Every effort has been made to contact copyright holders of any material reproduced in this book. Any omissions will be rectified in subsequent printings if notice is given to the publisher.

Contents

Some words are shown in bold, **like this**. You can find out what they mean by looking in the glossary.

What Is Dew?

Early in the morning, lawns, trees, and cars are sometimes wet. This can happen even when it has not rained. They are wet because of dew.

Tiny drops of water can cover things outside. These drops of water are called dew. Sometimes you can see them shining in the early morning sunlight.

Where Does Dew Come From?

Dew comes from water in the air. Water that is part of the air is called **water vapor**. At night, the ground and air get cooler. Then water vapor can turn into dew.

Air above the ground cools

Ground cools at night

Dew drops form

Dew does not fall from the sky like rain. The way dew forms is called **condensation**.

Dew can form on any cold thing, even a spider's web.

We cannot see the water in water vapor. When water vapor turns into dew, it becomes **droplets** of water that we can see.

What Is Frost?

Sometimes, frost looks a bit like snow.

After a very cold night, the ground can have a white covering of frost. A covering of frost is sometimes called hoarfrost.

Frost is made up of many tiny **ice crystals**. The crystals are **water vapor** that has **frozen**. They are so small that you can only see them clearly through a **microscope**.

In frost, each tiny ice crystal has a similar shape.

Where Does Frost Come From?

Frost can form on the ground and trees on cold days.

Like dew, frost comes from **water vapor** in the air. Frost forms when the air touches things that are very cold. The water vapor **freezes** into **ice crystals** on these cold things.

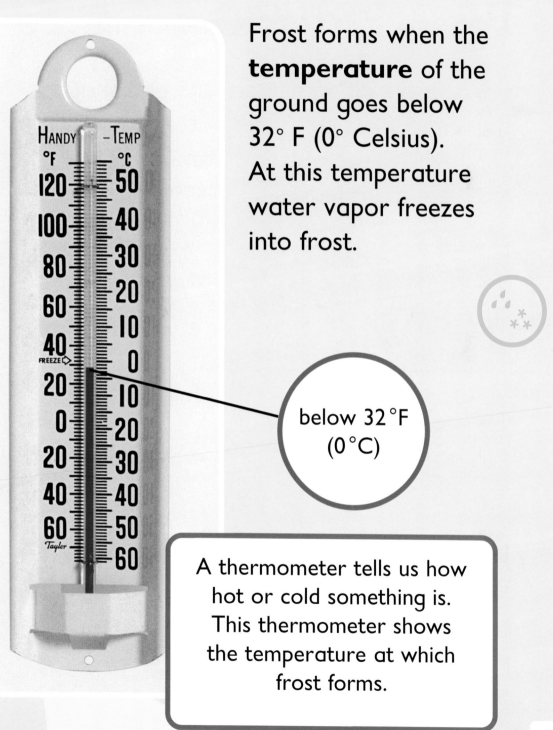

Frost forms when the **temperature** of the ground goes below 32° F (0° Celsius). At this temperature water vapor freezes into frost.

below 32°F (0°C)

A thermometer tells us how hot or cold something is. This thermometer shows the temperature at which frost forms.

HANDY — TEMP

°F   °C

120   50

100   40

80   30

60   20

          10

40   0

FREEZE

20   10

0   20

20   30

40   40

60   50

Taylor   60

Frosty Patterns and Shapes

Frost forms different patterns and shapes.
In winter, frost can form patterns on
windows. These patterns sometimes
look like plant leaves.

This is called fern frost. It
looks like the leaves of a
fern plant.

Rime is made of frozen water droplets from mist or fog.

Fog and mist can carry very cold **droplets** of water. When wind blows these droplets onto things that are below 32° F, they **freeze** into **ice crystals**. This type of frost is called rime.

Dew, Frost, and Animals

Dewdrops form on the beetle's back. When the drops run down a leg, the beetle can drink them.

Animals need water to live. In hot deserts there is very little water, so some animals drink dew to stay alive.

Animals can drink dew, but not frost. In frosty places, birds and other animals may not have any water to drink. They cannot drink the frost until it **melts** into water.

Frost is **frozen** water, so animals cannot drink it.

Dew, Frost, and Plants

Some plants live high up in **rain forest** trees. They cannot get water from **soil**, as most plants do. Instead, they take in dew, **water vapor**, or falling rain.

Plants need water to live. This plant collects dew in a cup formed by its leaves.

Evergreen trees with narrow, needle-shaped leaves are called conifers. Most conifers grow well in places where there is a lot of frost.

In frosty winter weather, the leaves on many plants die and drop off. Other plants have special leaves that can live through frosty weather.

Frosty Problems

Frosty, cold weather can cause all kinds of problems. In cold weather, we should keep ourselves warm by wearing a lot of clothes and by moving around.

Frost can make the ground slippery, so we have to walk carefully.

These winter crops are being grown under big plastic sheets. This saves them from the frost.

Frost can damage **crops**. Farmers sometimes protect crops from frost by using heaters or fires. These keep the ground and the air around the plants warm.

The Big Freeze

Driving fast on black ice causes accidents.

In very cold weather, frost or dew on roads may become a sheet of ice. This ice makes the road very slippery. It is called black ice because the black road shows through it.

Black ice is very dangerous because drivers cannot see it. On television and radio, **meteorologists** warn people about black ice.

Special trucks throw sand and salt onto roads to stop dangerous black ice from forming.

Is It Frost?

Freezing water can break rocks. This is called frost wedging. Although it has frost in its name, frost wedging is not caused by frost. It happens when water freezes in cracks.

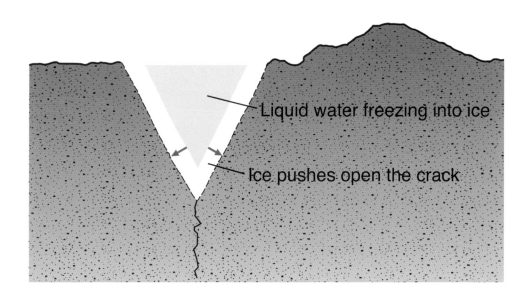

Liquid water freezing into ice

Ice pushes open the crack

As water freezes, it takes up more space and makes the crack bigger.

Frost wedging can make rocks fall. Mountain climbers wear helmets to help keep them safe.

Frost wedging happens a lot on mountains. It can break big rocks apart. The broken rocks often fall down the mountainsides.

Not Really Frost

These tomatoes have been damaged by black frost.

Black frost is not really frost. It is not made of **water vapor** that has **frozen**. Black frost forms when the water inside living plants **freezes**.

Frostbite is not caused by frost. It happens when part of someone's body freezes. People can lose their toes because of frostbite.

Mountaintops are very cold places. Mountain climbers must be warmly dressed, so they do not get frostbite.

Permafrost

Even though permafrost has the word *frost* in its name, it is not frost at all. Permafrost is **frozen** ground that stays frozen all year.

Trees do not grow in permafrost. Only grasses and other small plants can grow.

These people live in a very cold part of Canada where there is permafrost.

It gets very cold in places where there is permafrost. People must be very warmly dressed when they go outside.

Project: Water From the Air

This project shows you how to make your own drops of water from **water vapor**.

You will need:
- a soda can
- refrigerator
- warm room

1. Put a soda can in a refrigerator and leave it there for about three hours.

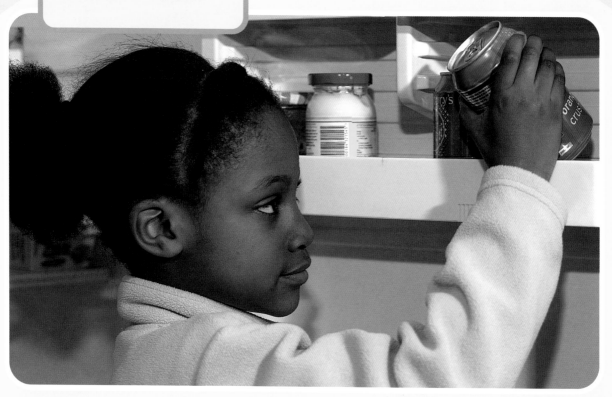

2. Take the cold soda can out of the refrigerator and put it in a warm room.

3. Watch what happens. Drops of water should form on the can.

4. Why do you think this happens?

What happens?

A warm room has a lot of water vapor in the air. The water vapor changes into drops of water when it touches the cold can. This is called **condensation**.

Glossary

condensation way water vapor turns into drops of water, or dew

crop plant that farmers grow, such as grains, vegetables, and fruit

droplet very small drop of a liquid, such as water

freeze turn into a very cold solid. For example, water freezes into ice.

frozen when water vapor or liquid water has turned into solid ice

ice crystal tiny bit of water that are frozen solid

melt turn from solid to a liquid. For example, ice melts into water.

meteorologist person who studies the weather and figures out what the weather might be like

microscope instrument to make small things look bigger, so we can see them better

rain forest jungle where a lot of rain falls

soil also called earth, mud, or dirt. Soil is made up of lots of different things, including tiny pieces of rock and dead plants.

temperature how hot or cold something is

water vapor tiny droplets of water that are part of the air around us. The droplets are so tiny and light that they can float in the air.

More Books to Read

Ashwell, Miranda and Andy Owen. *Watching the Weather*. Chicago: Heinemann Library, 1999.

Burke, Jennifer S. *Cold Days*. Danbury, Conn.: Scholastic Library Publishing, 2000.

Martin, Elena. *Hot or Cold?* Bloomington, Minn.: Capstone Press, 2003.

Royston, Angela. *Water*. Chicago: Heinemann Library, 2001.

Index